I0828950

NONE LIKE CHRIST.

ET TENEO ET TENEOR.

BY

OCTAVIUS WINSLOW, D.D.,

Author of "Go and Tell Jesus," etc.

New-York:

ANSON D. F. RANDOLPH, 770 BROADWAY.

1868.

None Like Christ.

"WHAT is thy beloved more than another beloved?"—SONG SOL. 5: 9.

THE power of *contrast* is acknowledged. The poet studies it in the construction of his epic; the artist in the coloring of his picture; the logician in the arrangement of his argument; the lover of nature as his eye roves over the outspread landscape—all are conscious of the presence and power of this principle. The object of contrast is not to create the ideal, or to foster the fictitious; but to confirm the existence, and highten the power and impression of the true. It is thus that the beautiful becomes more attractive, the grand more sublime, the good more excellent, and the object which awoke our admiration and inspired our regard, enthrones itself more firmly and supremely upon the soul.

The Word of God is replete with contrasts. In no volume is the effect more striking. How constantly, by an easy and graceful antithesis, the Holy Ghost places in contrast the vanity of idols, and the existence of God—the insignificance of man, and the greatness of Jehovah—the evanescence of things temporal, and the permanence of things eternal —the deformity of sin, and the beauty of holiness—the objects and attractions of earth, and the scenes and allurements of heaven —our waywardness and unworthiness, with God's long suffering and love. With what power, beauty, and reality are the great things of God's word thus brought out!

In presenting to you, my reader, the Lord Jesus Christ, as worthy of your undivided affection, supreme confidence, and unreserved service, infinitely distancing and eclipsing all other beings and all other objects brought in competition with him, we purpose adopting this principle; assured that the result must be, with the accompanying blessing of the Holy Spirit, the supreme enthronement of Christ in your admiration, trust, and love, as the "*chief among ten thousand, and the one altogether lovely.*" Happy shall we be if the conviction of the truth is deepened in your soul, NONE LIKE CHRIST!

Nor could we engage your thoughts upon a subject more suitable to the new and solemn period of time upon which we have entered. You are about to add another deathless chapter to the momentous volume of your personal history. As yet its lines are untraced, its events unrecorded. What that history may be, you have no prescience to guide your knowledge; nor, if you are wise and trusting, do you wish to know—calm and fixed in the assurance that it is all prearranged in the covenant that is "*ordered in all things, and sure;*" and that, impenetrable as is the vail that conceals it from your eye, God will permit nothing to transpire but what he has shaped and tinted with just that form and hue that will the most perfectly harmonize and blend, and will the most surely promote, your greatest well-being with his highest glory.

The Beloved.

"*What is thy beloved more than another beloved?*" It is clear, from this interrogation, addressed to the Church of Christ, that other and rival beings, other and competing objects, were brought into comparison with Christ, asking, if not a superior, yet an equal share of homage and regard; and the Church is challenged to a vindication of the higher and superior attractions claimed for her beloved Lord. "*What is thy beloved more than another beloved?*"

It is a humiliating fact, that there exists no object, the most trivial and contemptible, which the unrenewed mind will not place in competition with, and choose in preference to, and delight in to the exclusion of the Lord Jesus Christ! Take a brief and summary view of these claimants to man's regard—these rivals of Christ—and see how far they are worthy of a moment's consideration, when brought in contrast with the incarnate Son of God. Before we proceed, however, to particularize, let us premise that this is no new phase or development of our depraved humanity. Our world has ever been a Christ-rejecting world. From the moment the angels' song broke in music upon the plains of Bethlehem, the prediction of the Christ-exalting prophet, Isaiah, commenced its sad fulfillment: "*He is despised and rejected of men.*"

With some individuals, *self* is the rival — self in some of its many forms. Self-righteousness, self-seeking, self-indulgence, self-worship is the acknowledged and enthroned god, the "beloved" object of the unrenewed mind's supreme affection and worship. With others, the *world* is preferred to Christ — its acquisitions, opinions, and pleasures. O treacherous world! what myriads hast thou drawn within thy insatiable vortex, "drowning men's souls in perdition!" Reader, art thou preferring its gayeties, its riches, its honors, its religion to Christ? Pause on the threshold of this solemn period of time, and ask: "What, should I die this year, will the world I have chosen in preference to the Saviour do for me when eternity stares me in the face?" Others place the *creature* in competition with Christ; the creature and not the Saviour is their "beloved." But what a fearful crime are they chargeable with, "*who worship and serve the creature more* (or rather) *than the Creator, who is blessed forever.*" The creature is the defaced, the spoiled image of God. To prefer this marred and ruined temple to the glorious Being who constructed it, is to place yourself upon a level with the idolatrous Persian, who in his blindness worships the sun as the image of the Deity. But what superior excellence and attraction has an earthly beloved, that you should choose, love, and adore it in preference to the Heavenly One, who, as human, is "*fairer than the children of men*," and who, as divine, is "*God over all, blessed for evermore*"? God will not hold him guiltless who loves, worships, and serves the creature rather than the Creator. Thus, there is nothing earthly, mean, and contemptible which the natural man will not place above God, and prefer to Christ. His estate, his rank, his talents, his reputation, his very person, is "*made to sit in the temple of God, showing itself that it is God*," receiving the incense of adoration and worship, which alone belongs to Jehovah.

Reader, whatever earthly object reigns *supreme* in your mind and affections, dethrones and supplants the Lord Jesus. It may be your daily calling, or some pleasure of memory, or some object of taste — music, sculpture, painting, literature, science — whatever the master-passion of your soul, the supreme, all-engrossing object of your life, it is your Christ, your Saviour, your beloved, your all; and with this, your only portion and preparation, you are, in a little while, to confront the bar of God! "*Where your treasure is, there will your heart be also.*" But we approach yet closer our subject, and proceed to unfold the preëminent place Christ occupies in the universe of life, beauty, and love—in the world of nature and of grace—showing that there is not, amidst this vast assemblage of magnificent objects and glorious beings, one like Christ.

"None like Christ!" How familiar is this sentiment to the family of God. Sometimes it is the expression of gladsome joy, at others, breathed in sadness and in grief. When some beam of holy rapture has lighted up the soul, and the preciousness of the Saviour is felt, then the tongue exclaims, "None like Christ!"—no joy like that which Jesus inspires! Or, when some scheme of human happiness is blighted, some cherished friendship chilled, some idol god smitten from its shrine, some earthly spring dried, turning from the scene, spirit-wounded, heart-saddened, and disappointed, the soul has fled anew to Christ, its true attraction and rest, and with a depth of emotion and an emphasis of expression, the inspiration only of such a feeling, the believer has exclaimed: "Lord, there is none like thyself! I learn thy transcendent worth, I experience thy matchless love, I behold thy unrivaled beauty, I feel thy inimitable tenderness, gentleness, and sympathy in this hour when my spirit is overwhelmed within me, and my earthly treasures float a scattered wreck upon the surging waters through which I come to thee!" But follow us, dear reader, while, in a few particulars, we attempt to justify the preeminence of the Saviour, and establish your believing soul in the truth that "*there is none like Christ!*"

No Glory like His.

We begin with the statement, *that there is no glory like Christ's glory.* The universe is full of glory, because it is full of God. But God designed that his Son should occupy a place among created intelligences equal to himself touching his divinity, and inferior to himself only as touching his humanity; and both, mysteriously combined, constituting him "*the head of all principalities and powers;*" and, "*that all men should honor the Son, even as they honor the Father,*" of whose glory Christ is the effulgence, and of whose substance Christ is the exact impress. The deep gloom of earth was never illumined with such a light as when the Son of God descended from heaven; and the brightness of heaven never shone forth with such a lustre as when he returned back from earth, invested with the sinless robe of our nature—the divine prophet—the atoning priest—the triumphant king.

Marvel not that all the hierarchies of heaven bend low before that central throne on which sits the glorified Redeemer, and that at his feet the elders cast their crowns. Surely, it is the wonder and the glory and hallelujah of heaven, that divinity could stoop so low, and not be less divine;

and that humanity could rise so high, and not be less human. Oh! there is no glory like Christ's glory. Reader, can you, with the exulting Evangelist, exclaim: "*We have seen his glory, the glory of the only-begotten of the Father, full of grace and truth.*" Judge of the sacred vision by its hallowed effects. "*We all, with open face beholding as in a glass the glory of the Lord, are changed into the same image from glory to glory, even as by the spirit of the Lord.*"

This transforming, sanctifying influence of Christ's surpassing glory is real and palpable. One beam darting into your heart will pale the glory of the world, the glory of the creature, and the glory of self. And when this divine sun has risen resplendent on your soul—a child of darkness though you are—a worm of earth hiding in your obscurity and gloom—you may emerge from your cloistered solitude and woe, bask in its warmth, sun you in its effulgence, and exult that, as a pardoned sinner, a justified believer, an adopted child, all this glory of Christ's is *yours*—your robe of righteousness and your diadem of beauty — constituting you a king and a priest unto God. Oh! rest not, beloved reader, until this divine light is come, and the glory of the Lord is risen upon you. Then, and not till then, will you arise and shine in the beauty of holiness, a child of the light shedding its lustre all around you; and henceforth, whatever be the leadings of your Saviour, or the dealings of your God, the way along which he conducts you, checkered, winding, lonely, will be that of the "*just, which is as the shining light which shineth more and more unto the perfect day.*"

No Beauty like His.

Another observation naturally results from this—*there is no beauty like Christ's beauty.* We might expect that such divine glory, if ever it tabernacled on earth—the world's resplendent Shekinah—would be enshrined in a temple in all respects worthy of its dignity. We therefore find language like this: "*When he cometh into the world he saith, sacrifice and offering thou wouldst not, but a body hast thou prepared me.*" It was a body prepared by the Holy Ghost, of real, yet sinless flesh, in which the Son of God was to dwell. Hence we find the inspired artist, in portraying Christ's beauty as man, represents him as "*fairer than the children of men—grace is poured into thy lips.*" Himself the source and author of all beauty, his own beauty eclipses all. We love to trace the creations of his beauty, in the varied and endless forms of loveliness which still linger, adorning and enriching this fallen world. Those bright constellations — Christ created them; those burning suns — Christ kindled them; those snow-wreathed alps, those cloud-capped hills—Christ reared them; those verdant vales—Christ spread them; that blushing rose, that graceful lily, that exquisite fern, that curious sea-flower tossed upon the shore, that wayside violet that screens the dew-drop from the sun, that winding stream, that leafy grove — Christ formed and penciled it all. Christ clad that magnificent landscape with its robe of living green, scented the air with its fragrance, and hollowed out the depth of that expanding ocean dimpled with beauty by the gentle breeze, or awful in its grandeur when trod by the giant storm. Truly, "*he hath made every thing beautiful in his time.*" Oh! I delight to see the incarnate God, who died to save, scattering from the opulence of his own boundless resources all this jewelry, making man's sinful home so rich, so lovely, so attractive. But his own beauty, who can describe it? His person so lovely, his nature so holy, his heart so fond, his spirit so gentle, his look so winning, his voice so soothing. His whole character, life, and demeanor so inlaid and resplendent with every human, spiritual, and divine perfection — truly, it was no imaginative picture, and it was no mere oriental imagery with which the Church, in her just and lofty conception, described him as the "*Chief among ten thousand, and the altogether lovely.*"

But Christ's beauty is *shared* with all those who have union with him. Washed in his blood, robed with his righteousness, and adorned with his graces, each believer is comely, through his comeliness put upon him. And there is more of wonder, because there is more of God, there is more of beauty, because there is more of Christ, in that poor sinner who clings in penitence, faith, and love to the cross, looking up to God as a pardoned child, and pulsating with a life derived from the indwelling spirit, than in all this vast creation, enameled and sparkling with endless forms of loveliness. Reader, has Christ's beauty caught your eye, and penetrated your soul, transforming you into a sun-picture, reflecting his image in your Christ-like principles, your Christ-like spirit, your Christ-like walk, your whole Christ-like life? Then, dim and imperfect as is the copy, ere long it will be complete, when you "*shall see the King in his beauty*," and join the faultless throng who encircle the throne of God and the Lamb. Oh! then, be it your employment to contemplate, study, and reflect the beauty of Christ, for there is no beauty like his! "It is a finished portrait!" exclaimed an accomplished infidel, as the character of Christ was delineated to his view. It *is* a finished portrait; examine it, transfer it to yourself, and beware how you allow a creature's beauty—a being of human loveliness and love—to vail or shade a scintillation of Christ's surpassing beauty from your eye.

No Love like His.

There is no love like the love of Christ. The association of con trast will aid us here. God, who is love, is the author of all human affection. Love is the creation of Deity, the descendant of heaven, the reflection of God; and he whose soul is the most replete with divine love is the most like God. Paralyzed though our humanity is by the fall, tainted as it is by sin, the human heart is still the home of love in some of its loftiest and purest forms. It is impossible to behold its creations without the profoundest reverence. Who can stand, for instance, in the presence of a *mother's* love and not be awed by its dignity, won by its power, and melted by its tenderness?

But there is a love which equals, a love which excels, a love which surpasses it — it is the love of Christ! Institute your contrast. Select from among the different relations of life, the nearest and dearest; choose from those relations the deepest, purest, truest love that ever warmed the human breast, prompting to generous and noble deeds, to tender and touching expressions, to costly and precious sacrifices, and place it side by side with the divine love that chose you, the love that ransomed you, the love that called you, the love that soothes you, the love whose eyelid never closes, whose accents never change, whose warmth never chills, whose hand is never withdrawn — "*the love of Christ which passeth knowledge*" — and it is the very inspissance of selfishness, the frost of coldness itself. The love of Christ stands out in the history of the affections the divinest, the holiest, the strongest of all love, unequalled, unparalleled, unsurpassed. Oh! there is no love like Christ's love! Trace its features.

THE LOVE OF CHRIST IS A REVEALING LOVE. It uplifts the vail from the heart of God, and shows how that heart loves me. I had known nothing of the love of my Father in heaven, but for the love of my Saviour on earth. And that penitent, believing soul that feels the softest, gentlest pulse of Christ's love throbbing in his breast, knows more of the heart of God, sees more of the glory of God, and understands more of the character of God, than were earth and sky and sea to collect all their wonders and lay them at his feet.

THE LOVE OF CHRIST IS A CONDESCENDING LOVE. No other love ever stooped like Christ's love. Go to Bethlehem and behold its lowliness, and as you return, pause awhile at Gethsemane, and gaze upon its sorrow, then pursue your way to Calvary, and learn, in the ignominy, in the curse, in the gloom, in the desertion, in the tortures, in the crimson tide of that cross, how low Christ's love has stooped. And still it stoops! It bends to all your circumstances. You can be conscious of the becloudings of no guilt it will not cancel, of the pressure of no sin it will not lighten, of the chafings of no cross it will not heal, of the depths of no sorrow it will not reach, of the dreary loneliness of no path it will not illumine and cheer. Oh! is there a home on earth where the love of Christ most loves to dwell, where you will oftener find, yea, always meet it? It is the heart-broken, contrite, and humbled for sin!

THE LOVE OF CHRIST IS A SELF-SACRIFICING LOVE. "*Christ hath loved us, and hath given himself for us, an offering and a sacrifice to God for a sweet-smelling savor.*" What a laborious life, what a suffering death was his, and all was but the out-paying, outpouring of his love. Every precept of the broken law he obeyed, every penalty of an exacting justice he endured. The path that conducted him from Bethlehem to Calvary wound its lonesome way through scenes of humiliation and insult, of trial and privation, the storm growing darker and darker, the thunder waxing louder and louder, and the lightning gleaming brighter and brighter, until its central horrors gathered round the cross and crushed the Son of God! O marvelous love of Christ! what more couldst thou do than thou hast done? To what lower depth of ignominy couldst thou stoop? what darker sorrow couldst thou endure? Where did another cross ever impale such a victim, or illustrate such love?

NOR IS THERE ANY LOVE SO FORGIVING AS CHRIST'S LOVE. Forgiveness of injury is an essential element of true affection. We see not how it can exist at the same moment and in the same breast with an unbending, unrelenting, unforgiving spirit. Real love is so unique and lofty a passion, so Godlike and divine in its nature and properties, we can not conceive of it but in alliance with every ennobling, elevating, and worthy sentiment. Selfishness, malignity, revenge, uncharitableness, and all evil speaking, are passions of our fallen and depraved humanity, so hateful and degrading, it would seem impossible that they should exist for an instant in the same atmosphere with *true* affection. But a yet loftier form, a more sublime embodiment of love is presented to us in the love of God which is in Christ Jesus. God can not love—we speak reverently—and not *forgive.* Those whom God loves, God pardons. That God regards every individual of the fallen race with a feeling of *benevolence*, is unquestionable; "*for he maketh his sun to rise on the evil and on the good, and sendeth rain on the just and on the unjust;*" but those to whom the *love* of God extends, his everlasting, especial, and redeeming love—the gracious, the full, the eternal *forgiveness* of all sin likewise extends. God could not *love* a being and make that being over into the hands of a stern, avenging justice. Divine love will never lose the meanest and unworthiest object of its affections.

If, my reader, you feel conscious that you love God, though your affection be but as a smouldering ember, as a glimmering spark, be ye sure of this, that God *first* loved you; and loving, he has pardoned you; and pardoning, he will preserve you to his heavenly kingdom, that you may behold his glory, and enjoy his presence forever.

We repeat the remark, there is no love so forgiving as Christ's love. A human love may for an instant hesitate and falter; it may dwell upon the wrong inflicted, the injury done, the wound still bleeding; may, in its very muteness, speak in tones of inexpressible sadness, of confidence betrayed, of feelings lacerated, of friendship sported with, and the heart may find it difficult to take back the wrong-doer — the offender forgiven and the offense forgotten — to its embrace. But not so Jesus; he has canceled, obliterated, erased every shadow of a shade of his people's sins, and they shall come no more into remembrance. "*Then came Peter to him, and said, Lord, how oft shall my brother sin against me, and I forgive him? till seven times? Jesus saith unto him: I say not unto thee until seven times; but until seventy times seven.*"

Contrast this love, my reader—the forgiving disciple, the forgiving Saviour—and then exclaim: "*Who is a God like unto thee, that pardoneth iniquity, and passeth by the transgression of the remnant of his heritage? He retaineth not his anger forever, because he delighteth in mercy.*" There is no love, too, so gentle, so patient, so enduring, as Christ's love. Again and again you have questioned it, wounded it, forsaken it; again and again you have returned to it with tears, confession, and humiliation, and have found it as unchilled and unchanged as his nature. It has borne with your doubts, has been silent beneath your murmurings, has vailed your infirmities, and has planted itself a thousand times over between you and your unseen and implacable foe. It has never veered with your fickleness, nor frozen with your coldness, nor upbraided you for your backslidings, but all the day long, tracking your wandering, winding way, it has hovered around you with a presence that has encircled you within its divine, all-enshrouding, and invincible shield.

Truly, there is no love like Christ's! Nor is there any love that so chimes with human grief as his. Born in sorrow, schooled in adversity, baptized in suffering, acquainted with grief in its every shape, it is just the love for which our sorrows pant. There is but *one* heart in this vast universe that can meet your case, O child of affliction! it is the divine yet human heart of Christ. All other love and sympathy, the most intense and feeling, touches but the surface of our grief. Its trembling hand often irritates the wound it seeks to cicatrize; or, perchance, from the very intensity of its sympathy, catches the contagion of our grief, and sinks at our side helpless, hopeless, and despairing. Then it is the love of Christ approaches, touches us, and we are healed; speaks to us, and all is peace.

> "O unexampled love!
> Love nowhere to be found, less than divine."

How much of sacred meaning is contained in the prayer breathed by Paul on behalf of the Thessalonian saints: "*The Lord direct your hearts into the love of God.*" The image is expressive. You have often, doubtless, trodden in pensive thought the sands which belt some expanded ocean, when the tide has ebbed, and have marked the undulating surface of reef and shallow that has traced and disfigured it. You have revisited the spot when that tide has rolled back in its majesty and fullness, and lo! not a vestige of the former scene appeared; every shallow is filled, every line of blemish is erased, and the blue waves toss their jocund heads as gracefully and musically as ever. Such is the love of Christ! When this divine ocean recedes from your soul, you are filled with dismay at the spectacle that appears of emptiness, barrenness, and deformity. The love of Christ in the soul depressed, *all* is depressed. That ebbing tide has borne upon its receding wave the heart's last throb of gladness, and the soul's last gleam of hope, and nothing meets the eye but spiritual aridness and sin. Alarmed at the sad picture, you are roused to prayer, and you cry: "*Restore unto me the joys of thy salvation.*" Your petition is accepted, and the response is heard, "*I am returned to Jerusalem with mercies;*" and once more Christ's love flows back in gentle wavelets upon your soul, vailing every infirmity, and naught but the sweetest melody breathes from your heaving bosom.

No Saviour like Him.

There is no Saviour like Christ. Sin is inventive; itself the greatest invention of all. It is Satan's infernal machine for destroying precious souls by the million. In nothing is his ingenuity and power more put forth than in constructing expedients of salvation other than the atoning sacrifice of the Lord Jesus Christ. But Jesus is the one and only Saviour of men; "*neither is there salvation in any other; for there is none other name under heaven given among men whereby we must be saved.*"

It is the glory of Christ's salvation that it is perfectly adapted to every condition of our fallen and helpless humanity. Christianity is the only religion that fully recognizes the natural and utter depravity of our nature, and our consequent impotence to save ourselves. Jesus, therefore, is the

Saviour of *sinners.* He has undertaken to save us just as we are. He finds us a ruin, and recreates us; he finds us fallen, and raises us up; he finds us guilty, and he cleanses us; he finds us condemned, and he justifies us; all our salvation is in him. All the merit God requires, all the help man needs, all the grace and strength our salvation demands, dwells in infinite fullness in Christ.

My reader, your everlasting future of happiness or of woe depends upon your acceptance of Christ as your Saviour! Compared with this, your vital union with the Lord Jesus, churches are nothing, sacraments are nothing, religious duties are nothing, rites and ceremonies are nothing, because Christ must be *all* in the momentous matter of your everlasting well-being. Nothing saves you but faith in Christ, and, possessing that faith, nothing shall condemn you. You may adopt the soundest creed, may join the most apostolic communion, and may observe the most rigid austerities, and yet not be a Christian. United by faith to Christ, you may be saved in any Church; separated from Christ, you can be saved in no Church; "*for other foundation can no man lay than that is laid, which is Jesus Christ.*"

What a Saviour, then, is Christ!

That there should be to us lost sinners *any* Saviour, is marvelous; but that there should be provided for us *such* a Saviour as Christ is, so divine and human, so atoning and gracious, so able and willing, distances all thought, and is above all praise. None will he reject, who come to him. Oh! it were impossible to exaggerate this statement. All thought droops, all words fail in their attempt to show *what* a Saviour Christ is to poor lost sinners. He saves to the *uttermost.* He saves from the lowest depth of ruin, from the loftiest hight of guilt, from the farthest limit of sin, from the utmost verge of the yawning precipice, from the very mouth of hell! "*Where sin hath abounded, grace doth much more abound.*"*

If, abjuring all human merit, bewailing and deploring all sin, you accept as a *free-grace* bestowment, the salvation Christ wrought in his soul's travail on the cross, you shall be saved! If you stay away from Christ, your *best righteousness* will not preserve you from the eternal pains of hell. If you humbly and believingly come to Christ, your *worst sins* will not exclude you from the everlasting joys and blessedness of heaven. But it is of the utmost moment that you clearly recognize the only character and the sole ground on which Christ will save you. He will only save you as a *sinner*, and on the ground of his *finished work*, his infinite merit, atoning blood, and righteousness. You must stand where stood the publican, must kneel where knelt the "woman that was a sinner," must feel with Saul of Tarsus, that you are the "chief of sinners," must look and appeal to him with the true penitence and simple faith of the dying malefactor, and you *shall* be saved!

Cling Closer to Him.

Believer in Jesus! cling closer and closer to the Saviour, for there is none like unto him! Let the life you live be a daily coming up out of self into Christ. Place no limit to your transactions with Jesus. As yet you have but touched the margin of his ocean-fullness, you have but tasted that he is gracious, you have but crept beneath the hem of his ample robe. Oh! let this year be one of *advance;* your motto, "*forward.*" The truth each day's history will but confirm you in is, "*There is none like Christ.*" The more you trust to, and the more you draw from him, the deeper and sweeter will be your conviction and experience of this. It is a truth he intends you shall *experimentally* learn. He will have you prize, and love, and serve him above and beyond all others. The process by which you reach this high and holy attainment may be trying, the path rugged and toilsome, the ascent steep and difficult; it may cost you many a severe pang, many a deep sigh, many a lonely tear, many a sad wrench; nevertheless, a clearer realization of this truth, "none like Christ, none so near, none so powerful, none so precious," will more than recompense for all. Christ, in the sufficiency of his love and grace, will come and fill the blank, and soothe the pain, and dry the tear, and you shall look up, and with more than a seraph's rapture exclaim: "*Whom have I in heaven but thee?*

and there is none upon earth that I desire beside thee."

No Teacher like Him.

There is no teacher like Christ. Upon this point we can venture but a single remark. The Anointed of God, it is his office to reveal to us the great things of the Gospel. We are truly and savingly taught only as we are taught by him. Thankful for human teachers, we yet must exclaim: "*Who teacheth like Christ?*" With immediate access to our minds, and a quick avenue to our hearts, by one text, by one trial, and by one circumstance of our history, he can, in a moment, bring us into the experience of the deepest and most spiritual truth. Who teaches with the authority, or with the skill, or with the patience and gentleness of Christ? Become his student, beloved reader, enter as a disciple his school, and the Holy Spirit, whose office it is to glorify Christ, will lead you into all truth. Oh! that this may be a year of deeper, more spiritual teaching! Oh! that we may know more of our own nothingness and insufficiency, and more of Christ's fullness, loveliness, and love! Lord! that which I know not, teach thou me, for who teacheth to profit like thyself?

No Friend like Him.

There is no Friend like Christ. Beloved, it is possible that having many friends, you want yet *one.* God has, perhaps, endowed you with a nature keenly susceptible, your heart expanding to the warm and genial influence of true friendship. There is in your breast the responsive power of love, yet yearning for its object. Or, perchance, the cold blast of sorrow has swept over the garden of your confiding affections, and the finest feelings of your nature, torn from the support to which they clung, lie broken, wounded, and bleeding. You yearn for a friend, in the wisdom of whose counsel, in the depth of whose affection, in the delicacy of whose sympathy, in the patience of whose endurance you can implicitly and ever rely, and from whose presence nothing for a moment separates. That friend is Christ! "*I call you not servants, but friends,*" is his gracious avowal of the relation. "*He is a friend that sticketh closer than a brother.*"

There is not a friend on earth who loves you with his affection, who compassionates you with his sympathy, or is so powerful, so faithful, so near to you as Christ. Human friends do, indeed, divide our cares and double our joys; but

Jesus does more. He takes all our cares upon himself, absorbs all our sorrows in himself, and makes all his joy our own. Let this be a year of closer friendship with Christ! Confide in his love, avail yourself of his power, and demean yourself worthy of so precious a relation. Beware, in your dealings with him, of distrust, of shyness, of cooled affection. Place in him your unquestioning confidence, and give him your undivided heart. Let not the sad memories of past fickleness and failure fling their dark shadows on the future, but enter upon that future surrendering yourself afresh to Christ as your best Friend. Oh! there is none like him. Leave him for a while, though you may, for others, you return to him again with a yet deeper conviction of his superiority, exclaiming: "I find no friend like Christ. No love soothes me no smile gladdens me, no voice cheers me, no arm supports me as his."

You are entering upon a year which must be one of human infirmity, toil, and trial. Remember your chief, your best, your only Friend took upon him all your human infirmities, is identified with all your social affections, and is acquainted with all your lonely sorrows. Now that he is elevated to the loftiest reach of purity, to the highest degree of dignity and glory, and that that heart, once the abode of overshadowing grief, is all sunshine now, but fits him all the more exquisitely as the all-powerful, all-helpful, all-loving, all-tender, ever-present Friend and companion of your homeward path to God. O Christ! thou ever hast been, thou art, and thou shalt ever be my Friend! In adversity, I will hide beneath thy sheltering wing; in sorrow, I will nestle within thy loving bosom; in weakness, I will entwine around thy upholding arm; in want, I will repair to thy boundless resources; in sickness, in languor, and in suffering, I will enfold around me thy all-divine, all-human, all-pervading, all-soothing sympathy—

> "And when I die,
> Receive me, I'll cry,
> For, Lord, thou hast loved me,
> I can not tell why."

No Service like His.

And what *service* can be placed in competition with the *service of Christ?* The profession of Christian discipleship involves *a service.* The Christian life must needs have scope for the unfolding of its powers, and a field for the employment of its energies. But for the *activity* of Christianity our religion would become paralyzed and bedwarfed. It is a wise and merciful arrangement of its Author, that for the vital forces—the muscle and nerve and life of our Christianity — there should be provided a sphere ample and appropriate for their full development and play. The graces implanted in the soul — graces instinct with all the energy and power of the divine, before whose invincible might the fiercest assaults of the foe have been repelled, and the armies of the aliens put to flight — would become shriveled and collapsed, a moral atrophy seizing the whole soul, but for the *service* which summons them to action. Christ's kingdom supplies the appropriate and commanding sphere. The field of your exertion may be extended or circumscribed, just as God appoints. It may be the vast amphitheatre encircled by a great crowd of witnesses, gazing intently and anxiously upon your wrestling with sin and your battle with error; or, it may be some shaded nook, secluded from every eye, unaided and uncheered by human sympathy. Perhaps the sacred inclosure of home, or the night-watches of a sick-room, or the self-denying task of instructing a rude and obtuse class in the simple elements of the Gospel—yet is it Christ's service which engages you, and as such, it is perfect freedom and exquisite delight. And truly there is no service to be compared with it — so ennobling, so satisfying, so joy-inspiring — or that brings with it so much of present and rich reward. Servant of Christ! keep good heart! Listen to thy Master's feet behind thee, upholding and cheering thee on. He will soon come and pay thee thy full wages —will wipe the sweat of toil from thy brow, and wreathe it with an amaranthine crown of glory, honor, and immortality. Then comes the welcome and reward: "*Well done, good and faithful servant, enter thou into the joy of thy Lord.*"

With such a service, and such a recompense, who, with but a glow-spark of the love of Christ in his heart, will not exclaim: "*Here, Lord, am I, what wilt thou have me to do?*" I have but one life—thou hast bought it with thy life-blood—be it thine, thine wholly, forever thine." Christian reader, be up and doing—why stand ye all the day idle? Go, work in your Lord's vineyard. With a significance more profound, and with an earnestness more intense than that with which the words were uttered by the Mohammedan chief, pointing his sword to earth and then up to heaven, would we say to you: "*Here* is the place of labor; *there* is the place of rest."

"'Tis not for man to trifle; life is brief,
And sin is here;
Our age is but the falling of a leaf,
A dropping tear.
We have no time to sport away the hours;
All must be earnest in a world like ours.

"Not *many* lives, but only *one* have we;
One, only one:
How sacred should that one life ever be—
That narrow span!
Day after day filled up with blessed toil,
Hour after hour still bringing in new
spoil."

No Friend like Him.

The truth upon which we have been endeavoring to concentrate your thoughts, and with which we would yet a few moments longer detain you, is one of great *practical* influence. It chimes with every event, circumstance, and exigence of your life. Let your faith deal with it as a divine verity, as a practical reality, that in whatever position God places you, he intends, by his dealings in providence, and by his teaching in grace, to bring you into the deeper experience of this the most precious of all experimental and practical truths—"No one can meet my case like Christ."

Whatever, through this year, your position may be—and I will hypothetically place it—let faith reason thus: "I am in great adversity; why should I resort to the help of man, he may fail me—*there is none like Christ.* I am in profound grief, my heart is melted within me; why should I repair to the soothing of human sympathy, it may disappoint me —*there is none like Christ.* I am in a great strait; difficulties insurmountable, perplexities inextricable weave their network around my path, and I am at my wit's end; why should I betake me to human counsel, it may mislead me — *there is none like Christ.* My future looks dark and lowering—disease undermining my health—my energies failing, and the duties, responsibilities, and labors for which I have taxed my utmost powers, all lie untouched and neglected, yet why should I despond — *there is none like Christ.* My temporal circumstances are narrowing, resources fail me, penury, with its humiliating attendants, stares me in the face, yet why should I yield to unbelief—*there is none like Christ.* My corruptions are strong, my temptations irresistible, my sins many, my doubts and fears weigh me down to the dust, yet why should I despair — *there is none like Christ.* I am approaching the solemn hour of death, heart and flesh are failing me, and the vail of eternity is slowly rising to my view, yet why should I fear, and tremble, and shrink back, I have committed my soul to my

Saviour, and — *there is none like Christ.*" And, oh! what a mercy that you have never found one that could for a moment take his place; that, separated, perchance exiled from all others, you are inclosed to Christ alone, nor wish another being to share your confidence or divide your affection with him.

It is possible that you have made the experiment. You have traveled the circle of creation's good, have sipped at many springs, have gathered many flowers, have sought repose in many an embowered spot, but all have failed. You have returned to your true rest, exclaiming: "None like Christ. I find no love so soothing as his, no friendship so true, so gentle as his, no communion like communion with him. Christ is my all and in all." Does the world challenge: "*What is thy beloved more than another beloved?*" Your answer is at hand: "My beloved bore my sins, opened in his heart a fountain in which I am washed whiter than snow. My beloved sustains my burdens, counsels my perplexities, heals my wounds, dries my tears, supplies my wants, bears with my infirmities, upholds my steps, and cheers my pathway to the tomb. My beloved will be with me in the valley of the shadow of death, and with his presence I shall fear no evil. My beloved has gone to prepare a place for me in the many-mansioned house of my Father, and will come again and receive me to himself, '*that where he is, I may be also.*' My beloved will walk with me the gold-paved streets of the new Jerusalem, will lead me to fountains of living waters, and will wipe every tear from my eyes. *This* is my beloved, and *this* is my Friend!"

Therefore Stand Firm.

And yet have we need of constant vigilance, lest we should not always and in every thing give Christ the preëminence. The rival interests, and the antagonistic forces of the world and the flesh are in perpetual play. These demand that, with the prophet, we should "stand continually upon the watch-tower in the day-time, and be set in our wards whole nights." Should you discover any encroachment of your worldly calling upon the claims Christ has to your time and service, any rival affections to the claims he has to your whole heart, any secret demur to the claims he has to your unreserved obedience, should you, in a word, detect the undue ascendency or influence of any one being or object whose presence and power tends to shade the beauty, lessen the attractions, weaken the supremacy, or share the throne of Christ in your soul, that being and that object must be relinquished at once and forever. Oh! what competitor can stand side by side with Christ? No minister, or pastor, or church, or friend, or companion, can bear a moment's comparison with Jesus. Not one who can assist you, defend you, provide for you, or bear with you as he, who when the snow-flakes of wintry adversity fall thick and fast, and its cold blast moans drearily around you, will not quit your side, who will be first to enter the house of woe, across whose threshold the loved remains have just been borne, to speak words of comfort to your bereaved heart; who will sustain you in languor, bend over you in sickness, and when the last look, ere the eye is fixed and glazed, and the last breath, ere the lips are mute and immovable in death, shall come, will be with you, viewless and noiseless to the attendant watchers, sustaining your spirit in the parting hour, then bearing it in his own warm bosom to the home eternally made ready. Then cling and adhere to Christ, and in all things give him the preëminence.

> "Enthrone the precious Saviour in thine heart,
> Let all thine homage unto him be paid;
> Suffer no idol to usurp in part
> The glory due to him who all things made.
> In thought, word, deed, thy life to him be given,
> Thou shalt be blessed on earth, and saved in heaven."

Be Faithful to His Word.

There is yet another caution I would venture to give in reference to some of the social and popular movements of the day, the tendency of which, without due vigilance on the part of the sincere and earnest friends of true religion, may be adverse to its best interests, fatally injurious to the individuals contemplated by these movements, and subversive of the supremacy of Christ and his truth. We hail with gratitude and hope all efforts to advance "social science" and intellectual improvement, *provided* those endeavors are sustained and sanctified by Christian principle. I am thoroughly convinced that true national advancement can only be successfully secured by the power of a *living Christianity*. All other modes of elevating the masses utterly fail of reaching them. It is impossible to close the eye to the fact that, after all the exertions of our literary and scientific institutions, our libraries, reading-rooms, and lectures, there teems outside and far beyond our efforts, a vast outlying population of living beings, dwelling in ignorance and neglect, each one of whom might give utterance to the exclamation: "No man hath cared for my soul!" By what agency are we to compass and by what means are we to instruct them? We at once answer, by the feet of the city and the rural missionary, and by the sole instrument of Christ's Gospel. But widely different from this is the object promoted by "social science" and its kindred associations. And what is the result? We are advancing in secular knowledge and science, but, at the same time, we are equally advancing in worldliness, luxury, and indulgence; in extravagance of dress, and modes of life that, in numerous cases, far overlap reasonable and legitimate income. The consequences must be serious!

The history of nations is luminous in the testimony it bears to the fact that, high perfection in art and science, in intellectual improvement, luxury, and indulgence, apart from the conservative influence of Christianity, has ever been the culminating point that has marked their decadence and dissolution. We have passed through one phase of our national history, and "hero-worship" is near giving place to the worship of "social science," secular knowledge, and intellectual advancement.

I can not look but with the most painful apprehension and alarm upon the *unchristianized* condition toward which we are as a nation fast drifting. Compromise at home, and neutrality abroad, is gradually blotting Christianity from our national escutcheon. It seriously behoves the ministers of the Gospel, our devout statesmen and senators, to be broad awake. If we are to retain the position God has given us in the scale of nations, or to rise to a yet loftier altitude of moral greatness and power, it will not be by the means of social science,. worldly knowledge, wealth, luxury, and refinement, but by the influence of a living, vitalizing Christianity alone! The Bible and its religion must be paramount; Christ and his Gospel must have the preeminence. Reason and learning must stand at the bar of Revelation, reverence its dicta, adopt its principles, and obey its voice. The moment that finds this nation glorying in her strength, in her wisdom, in her wealth, in her prowess, in her social progress, and in her high civilization, will date the beginning of her decline, and foreshadow the certainty of her downfall as a great, religious people; and her last and latest history, like that of Greece and Rome, will be written in mourning, lamentation, and woe. Let the apostles and promoters of social science and of secular knowledge solemnly *beware* how, in the advancement of their objects, they ignore our Bible and abjure our God!

Be Spiritually Minded.

It is an important practical deduction from the subject of these pages, that if true godliness be any thing to us, it surely must be *every thing*. There is no principle God has more closely and universally studied in the universe than *harmony*. And it is this nice adjustment, this perfect balance, and exquisite symmetry, every where pervading his works, which proves the mind that planned and the power that executed to be one and the same — divine. Now it is this same harmony, as exhibited in true godliness, which illustrates its beauty and augments its power. How much is true religion shorn of its strength by the want of more *spiritual-mindedness* in its professors! The worldly amusements to which many addict them selves—the opera, the card-playing, the ball, the gay party, the novel-reading, the luxurious living, the extravagant customs in which multitudes of religious professors, church-members and communicants indulge, are sad blots upon their avowed Christianity, and effectual hindrances to the advancement of religion in their own souls and in the world. Oh! that with us vital religion — the pure, simple, self-denying, unearthly religion of Christ —

might be paramount; its holy influence permeating our whole being, and giving form and tint and direction to all our engagements and conduct. Difficulties we shall, indeed, have to overcome in the world, and, perchance, opposing influences in our own homes; nevertheless, if Christ see that our hearts are set upon ruling our lives by his divine precept, "*Seek ye first the kingdom of God and his righteousness,*" he will aid our holy strivings and vouchsafe his grace that, in our principles, our spirit, and our conduct, yea, in all things and every where, Christ may have the preëminence.

My reader, what is *your* "beloved"? If it is not Christ, what is it? The world? the creature? wealth? self? Are *these* the objects you place in competition with the Redeemer, and prefer to a religious life, a happy death, and a glorious eternity? Oh! what will they avail you when Christ, the Saviour you have slighted, despised, and neglected, cites you to his bar? Without the experience of a real conversion, of the new birth, of an interest in Jesus, should you die this year, you are forever lost! Pause, solemnly pause, upon the threshold of a new period of your probation, and ask the Holy Spirit to enthrone the Saviour upon your loving, believing heart, that *henceforth* Christ may be the first, Christ the chief, Christ preëminent; so that for you to live or die may truly and emphatically be CHRIST; and then Christ and you will be together through eternity.

There is None like Him.

Such is the truth, child of God, your heavenly Father has given you to learn through this coming year: *None like Christ!* Could he bring you into the experience of one more needful, more sanctifying, or more precious? Impossible! Strive after a closer walk, a more childlike transfer of every care, anxiety, and want to your heavenly Father, and his beloved Son, your elder brother. "*He careth for you.*" Do not overlook *to-day*, in your anxious thoughts about *the morrow.* Travel not out of the present into the future. The grace that succors, the love that comforts, the resources that supply to-day's need, will, with to-morrow's demand, be ready at your hand. Do justice to the solemn present, and live with the same calm reliance upon God, and looking to Jesus, as if there were but one second of time intervening between you and your heavenly home. Make the prayer your own of one of the earliest missionaries of the Cross to Ireland: "May the strength of God pilot me this day, the power of God preserve me, the wisdom of God instruct me, the eye of God view me, the ear of God hear me, the hand of God protect me, the way of God direct me, the shield of God defend me. Christ be with me, Christ before me, Christ after me, Christ in me, Christ under me, Christ over me, Christ at my right, Christ at my left, Christ at this side, Christ at that side, Christ in the heart of each person whom I speak to, Christ in the mouth of each person who speaks to me, Christ in each eye which sees me, Christ in each ear which hears me.

Salvation is the Lord's, salvation is Christ's. May thy salvation, O Lord! be always with us."* Imitating the spirit, and adopting the petitions of this remarkable prayer, your daily, happy, and holy experience and testimony will be: "None *but* Christ, none *like* Christ."

"I'll not leave Jesus — never, never!
Ah! what can more precious be?
Rest, and joy, and light are ever
In his hand to give to me.
All things that can satisfy,
Having Jesus, these have I.

* Called "St. Patrick's Armor;" a prayer on his going to preach before the King and States of Ireland. See *Church History of Ireland, by Rev. R. King, A.B.*

"Love has bound me fast unto him,
I am his, and he is mine;
Daily I for pardon sue him,
Answers he with peace divine.
On that rock my trust is laid,
And I rest beneath its shade.

"Without Jesus, earth would weary,
Seem almost like hell to me;
But if Jesus I have near me,
Earth is almost heaven to me.
Am I hungry? He doth give
Bread on which my soul doth live.

"Oh! how light upon my shoulder
Lies my cross, now grown so small!
For the Lord is my upholder,
Fits it to me, softens all.
Neither shall it always stay—
Patience! it will pass away.

www.ingramcontent.com/pod-product-compliance
Lightning Source LLC
LaVergne TN
LVHW011120110826
845150LV00008B/2201

* 9 7 8 1 4 2 5 5 0 4 7 8 6 *